"HERMAN, you were a much stronger man on our FIRST honeymoon."

by Jim

A Collection of HERMAN® Daily Panels

ANDREWS and McMEEL, INC.
A Universal Press Syndicate Company
KANSAS CITY • NEW YORK

ISBN: 0-8362-1117-0
Library of Congress Catalog Card Number:
83-71771

"Aw c'mon doc, let me borrow a mirror."

"I can't seem to make up my mind about this one!"

"Where are you hopping off to?"

"What was that cyclist shouting about back there?"

"If anyone needs me, Joyce, I'll be up on
the roof for about 20 minutes."

"Is it ten minutes to five already?"

"Quick, put it on. Someone's coming!"

"They don't allow those on my planet."

"Now I suppose you're gonna sulk because I wouldn't give you the afternoon off!"

"I'll have a coffee and a Danish to go."

"As I wasn't too busy, I made you my
international award-winning
hamburger-de-lux."

"I don't mind you reading over my
shoulder, but don't do the
crossword puzzle."

"Look, you're 103 years old, you've got to start taking better care of yourself."

"Your honor, before the jury retires to reach a verdict, my client wishes to present each of them with a little gift of jewelry."

"Have you got a 24-slice toaster?"

"Dad, a guy at school said we all came from humans."

"If you're so smart, how come the world was in such a mess before I got here?"

"You'd better remove your make-up. I've got some good news."

"I don't mind the 17th floor as long as I have 64 sheets."

"What did you *expect* to find in oxtail soup?"

"Will you keep the noise down! We're trying to have a party next door."

"Can you change a $100 bill?"

"Whad'dyer mean triplets! *He* was here first."

"I hate bothering you, but my wife wants to know if she passed her driver's test."

"I hope you know your stuff. I'm a very weak swimmer."

"I'll have to X-ray your arm again. This one is overexposed."

"Why did you move your plate?"

"According to the computer, we owe the gas company $14.3 billion for August."

"So this is Dotty, your wife."

"D'you mind if I take a photo? It's not often we get a 15-cent tip."

"Haven't you got one in English?"

"I hear you're looking for an aggressive salesman."

"I can't eat anymore of these turquoise peas!"

"You're the one who kept telling me you were a 'go-getter.'"

"Simpson, bring me an order of onion rings and move that candle further down the table."

"That was my ex-boyfriend's car!"

"Is it too tight across the shoulders?"

"I can't understand anyone being afraid of dogs."

"I'll have a cheeseburger and a root beer."

"Welcome to planet earth. Is your mother home?"

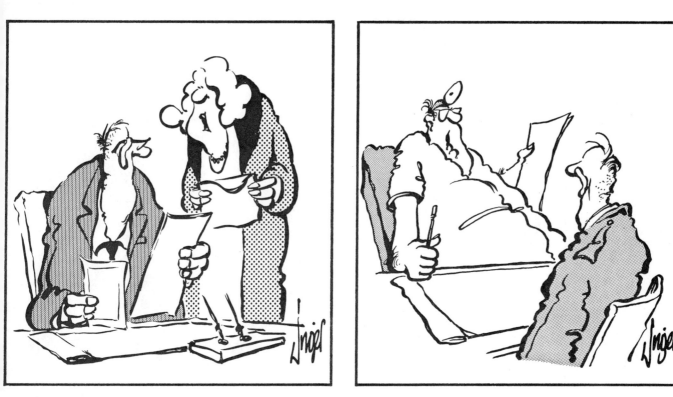

"I'm your new secretary. Am I an hour
late or 23 hours early?"

"It's a pity you're unemployed! You need
a couple of weeks off work."

"Your friend Muriel is going through
Harry's pockets again!"

"The mailman's been!"

"Whoever shouted 'Turkey' was correct."

"Now scrape that off the carpet and serve it to him on a clean plate."

"Remember your blood pressure!"

"Of course it's half eaten! You said you wanted the chef's salad."

"As soon as he's finished, rush that glass
of water over to table nine."

"Is the war over?"

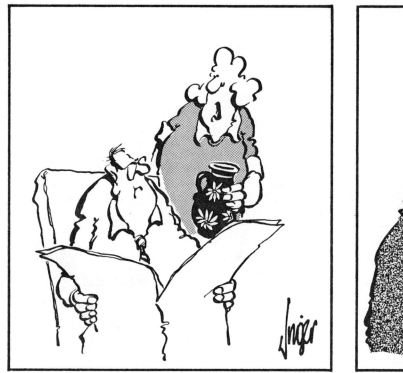

"All the cups are dirty. D'you want your coffee in that?"

"Be careful with the wine. I had trouble getting the cork out."

"Take that back! It tastes like the stuff my wife makes."

"Got a dog to fit that?"

"I lost the key for my padlock!"

"I wonder why they make these finger bandages so long?"

"I told you not to eat popcorn while you've got hiccups."

"Here's one you'll love! Two weeks in an open boat without food and water."

"I know it's your birthday soon, but what
can I buy a woman who has everything?"

"He's only been at his company for a year
and already he's getting the
minimum wage!"

"I was wondering how you'd play that shot."

"Ignorance of the law is no excuse, buddy!"

"How am I supposed to know you're
allergic to these if you don't tell me!"

"If you can spare the time, Williams, I'd
like to see you in my office."

"Gimme 14 hot hogs."

"Was he as short as that in real life?"

"In your case, we have no interest at all!"

"Cindy's getting a job at a bank and needs you as a reference."

"There's four billion of them down here! Make sure none get on the ship before we take off."

"Guy in the front row wants to know if you like blueberry or custard cream?"

"Coffee is 50 cents for the first half-hour and 30 cents for each additional half-hour."

"The top keeps flying off this food mixer."

"That robot that replaced you at work has been laid off!"

"I like the color but won't the water keep running out?"

"I think that dark shadow is where I
spilled some coffee."

"Can you cut me a star-shaped piece of
glass to fit that hole?"

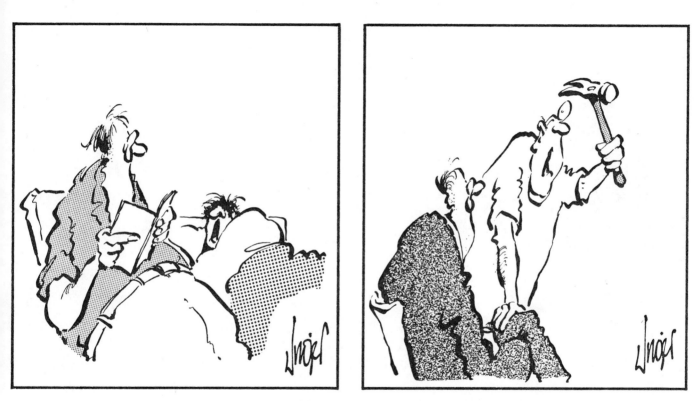

"You're supposed to read it aloud!"

"Nurse . . . see if you can find my little rubber hammer."

"Have you got any old bricks I can take to my karate lesson?"

"He wasn't always bald. It's acid rain."

"I asked him what he wanted for our anniversary and he said 'two minutes of silence.'"

"The doctor thinks he's going to be very musical."

"Okay, you've got the job! On your mark, get set, . . ."

"I think we've decided on the ruby-and-diamond cluster."

"Oh, Herman! You're my very first husband."

"Whaddyer mean, 'The strawberries aren't fresh'? I just opened the can five minutes ago!"

"Where did you put my book on
archaeology?"

"George, how many years have I been
coming in this candy store?"

"This wildlife book you sold me is nothing but animals!"

"I told you last week I had to work late tonight!"

"I don't really want a diagnosis. What diseases have you got for under $50?"

"This is your loan application back from our head office."

"204 lbs. on the left and 189 lbs. on the right."

"Look at that! 62 years old and not a single cavity."

"The TV keeps switching back to
'Wild Kingdom'!"

"I need a dishwasher that can handle
heavy, baked-on grease — three
times a day."

"If I didn't love you I wouldn't eat *this*, would I?"

"Did Grandpa give you permission to take that off his bad leg?"

"I've been at the hospital all day. My wife broke her fist."

"I knew he was really sick. He hasn't complained about anything for three days."

"She tries to watch what she eats but her eyes aren't quick enough."

"We've been happily married for two years — 1938 and 1945."

"Here . . . tell your mother we're out. She won't believe me."

"You had a hair transplant?"

"You won't find a job in the Sports section!"

"You can sit there 'til I find out where you hid my glasses!"

"This rascal chased the wife's mother 20 feet up a tree."

"You say you were inside robbing the bank and someone stole your car?"

"You wouldn't even have that job if my Grandpa hadn't got the flu."

"Mother sent us each a Christmas card."

"They dropped the speeding charge but I've got to pay for the three storefronts and the railway station."

"Here, work your way through that lot and I'll go easy on you next year."

"Fourteen shopping minutes
to Christmas!"

"This your idea of a good old-fashioned
Christmas — turkey pizza?"

"I'll take another bottle of this
after-shave."

"I told you not to lay in the bath
all afternoon!"

"That's the last time we'll use this hospital!"

"He wants to give us $1,000 to use the moon for a few days!"

"D'you buy used cats?"

"When are you going to face the fact
that you're a lousy pick-pocket?"

"That's $194.32, less four cents for the bonus coupon."

"We were just toying with the idea of going to see a movie. Can you come back in about three minutes?"

"This is a much bigger apartment than we're used to."

"Are we still hiring minorities?"

"I sold half the business!"

"I don't care if it *is* his birthday!"

"The judge gave my lawyer five years before he even got around to me!"

"Your honor, my client is the product of a broken home."

"The guy across the street wants to know what you're cooking."

"How long have you been on the
night shift?"

"If I get a good mark, you could be
looking at a very nice apple
tomorrow morning."

"It's my new slimming book."

"Can't you hum something else?"

"I can't hear the peasants singing. You'd better put the guard on 'red alert.'"

"Come on! Tell him you're sorry for stepping on him at the top of the stairs."

"We can't stand here all day. It must have jammed."

"I'm sorry, we're out of 'Multivitamins Plus Iron.'"

"Ralph, what's the price on these lizard's feet?"

"I'll skip the dessert menu. I don't like to run on a full stomach."

"Your honor, my client thinks ten years is a little harsh and requests permission to approach the bench."

"I won't be home Friday. They've changed all the locks."

"Up and left."

"I'm having a fabulous evening, but I really must be home by 8 o'clock."

"385 pounds, including the towel."

"I knew we shouldn't have bought waterfront property!"

"Do you have such a thing as a
refrigerator with a revolving door?"

"For the last time: I do not want
today's special."

"We had to remove your brain for a couple of days, so just try to relax."

"In 35 years, you're my first case of this!"

"I think we had much nicer diseases
when I was a girl."

"I've found a secret room!"

"Make sure he pays cash."

"Is that the man who tried to mug you?"

"This is the last one he painted."

"I'd ask you in, but I've only got one chair."

"Nurse, you'd better put these on."

"I see for the last **15** years you've been in financial management."

"Make sure he's home by 4 o'clock."

"She's here to get some entry forms for the Miss Universe competition."

"I've never told anyone before but I was aiming at a crocodile."

"We were wondering if we could extend the maximum limit on our charge account?"

"As soon as we got married I realized two can live as cheaply as six."

"How many times have I told you not to put your feet on the table?"

"I told you it was supposed to go around your neck."

"Can't you help me catch the canary?"

"You're looking at the next general manager of 'Louie's Take-Out Pizza.'"

"I just seem to be walking around in circles all day!"

"Old George has been with the company 38 years. Do I hear $300?"

"My daughter tells me you're hoping for a career in shipping."

"He jumped over 15½ buses!"

"He wants to sit with his back to the wall."

"Some of the guys at work are coming
over this evening to help me
do the dishes."

"Can't you take a joke?"

"It's part of our new policy of "preventive surgery.""

"He seems to have decided on a baseball scholarship."

"You wanna have good eyesight if you go abroad, don't you?"

"Just give him your money, dear. The last one sued us for his medical bills."

"Be careful how you try that one on, Madame. This is a very old building."

"She kept saying the dance floor was lumpy."

"I think you'll find my test results are a pretty good indication of your abilities as a teacher.

"Let me know immediately if you start feeling the urge to move sideways."

"I want you to take one of these with
water every four years."

"We were finding it very hot in
here, Warden."

"I would've been here sooner, but our iceberg hit a ship."

"Here's a nice shady spot over here!"

"Are you the guy who advertised he'd
found a wallet?"

"A whole boiled egg! So two years of
night school finally paid off."

"I think my memory's coming back! Ask me who won the World Series in 1998."

"As you can see, your insurance doesn't cover 'family squabbles.'"

"Arnold, will you please stand away from that on/off switch."

"I was halfway across the freeway and my hat blew off."

"I've lost the key!"

"He said he shot it in the desert."

"Remember Ralphy, the moron? He's making $250,000 a year."

"I'm sorry, sir, that's not hand luggage."

"Just relax and get your memory back. Don't lay there worrying about that $8 you owe me."

"Got a room with a panoramic view of the city?"

"I lost track of my age years ago, but I think I'm about 22."

"As we'll be flying over water, we present the following demonstration of what to do in the case of shark attack."

"I'd say that was just about a total eclipse, wouldn't you?"

"My wife would like to look at some fur coats. Got any binoculars?"

"This says you have a tendency to grovel.'

"And for the man who has everything, we have this personal nuclear deterrent."